Sama[...] pe[...]

For people [...]
other helpli[...]

Samaritans: Listening with people with Autism

Samaritans: Listening with people with Autism

Samaritans: Listening with people with Autism

Chapter 1 – Agitation

I just want to start and say that working as a samaritans volunteer probably isn't easy. You probably have to deal with a lot of calls coming in. You probably have to deal with a lot of things.

If someone with Autism is phoning up. Try to listen to their point of view. If they talk

Samaritans: Listening with people with Autism

about someone else. They are not phoning up for a chat. They are simply just making parallels in conversations. For example, sometimes I will reflect myself as similar to someone else.

The caller may not appear distressed. May have a calm voice. However, try to understand that there are underlying issues. Try to reach a mutual understanding of what the underlying issues are. They may be mute, appear quiet. Alternatively they may sound hyperactive. Try and be calm and avoid giving judgement. Even if you feel the call isn't genuine, always treat it as it is. As it's better to ear on the safe side of caution. I know lots of different people ring up The Samaritans. However, it's important to understand that very rarely would someone lie about having Autism.

If someone is appearing agitated with Autism. This is not to be confused with aggressive behaviour.

It's not personal. Agitation can be for multiple reasons. Personal issues. Anxiety issues. Any issues. Try to remain calm. Show

Samaritans: Listening with people with Autism

open body language. Avoid talking down to them. Don't swear, don't be sarcastic. Avoid being short, and at the same time. Say things in lamens terms to help them understand. Avoid any long jargon, especially if they are very anxious. Calm, asseertive and gentle reassurance.

Avoid sounding patronising or talking to them like a child. Talk to them like an adult, and try having some small talk/friendly banter with them along the way.

A lot of people with Autism repress emotions so if they appear okay. There may be hidden signs of distress that need to be looked out for.

I know volunteering in The Samaritans , with all types of work. Try to do a risk assessment on what you feel appropriate. Even if someone seems okay, there are sometimes underlying issues. Also due to the stigma of having mental health. There needs to be more understanding that sometimes an Autistic person may not want to talk. They may remain mute. This is called selective mutism.

Basically, sometimes they find it hard to talk or express themselves.

Samaritans: Listening with people with Autism

When I had written my book regarding giving The Police their refresher training on Autism. I was talking about hidden disabilities, and someone may not appear distressed. Even if they are. People with Autism are less likely to express their distress in ways, people without Autism would. So it's important to be patient. Show a non judgemental attitude. Be mindful if they are going off on tangents. That is just part of the condition.

Volunteering 4 hour shifts may be fast paced, you may have to be dealing with lots of calls. Make sure you meet them on a calm tone of voice and talk to them on their level. Show a non judgemental attitude, and be calm. Avoid to appear over bearing, and listen to them.

Listen to what they have to say, and if they are anxious or agitated. Try and be mindful and patient with them along the way. Try not to take what they are saying literally. As what I said. There may be hidden issues lying around. Underlying problems.

Samaritans: Listening with people with Autism

Samaritans: Listening with people with Autism

Show empathy and listen to their point of view. Don't humour them, and try to see things from their point of view. Try to understand things from how they feel.

Samaritans: Listening with people with Autism

Samaritans: Listening with people with Autism

Samaritans: Listening with people with Autism

Chapter 2 – Anxious behaviour

May appear anxious, but it is never personal and is always down to a reason to something either going on at home or having a bad day.

Samaritans: Listening with people with Autism

Try to sound calm. Sound confident, and don't try to show judgement.

Sound relaxed, and keep a calm tone of voice.

Even if you are feeling anxious. If you sound anxious, then this is going to put someone with Autism into feeling anxious also. Moods are contagious. So it's important to be calm. Deal with your own stresses on your own. Try not to project stresses onto people with Autism.

Samaritans: Listening with people with Autism

Samaritans: Listening with people with Autism

Samaritans: Listening with people with Autism

Samaritans: Listening with people with Autism

Samaritans: Listening with people with Autism

Samaritans: Listening with people with Autism

Samaritans: Listening with people with Autism

Samaritans: Listening with people with Autism

Samaritans: Listening with people with Autism

Samaritans: Listening with people with Autism

Samaritans: Listening with people with Autism

Chapter 3 – Caller may resort to innapropritate comments

Samaritans: Listening with people with Autism

The caller may say silly things, like "Look at this pink cloud." Or may laugh innapropriately. Or talk to themselves.

People with Autism are harmless, and sometimes you get innapropriate laughter. Or sometimes they may state the obvious. Try to show empathy towards them.

If they are super innapropriate, you may need to tell them politely that they shouldn't say it. However, be polite, and try making a joke out of a situation if it's light. If it's very rude, and aggressive. The slow, steady, and walking them towards a mutual solution. Is a good pace. You may not want to do this, however, if you meet them with aggression, they will become even more aggressive. Aggression in Autism is highly unlikely. Autistic people can become agitated, but aggressive, usually not.

Slow and gentle, calm, avoid looking down on them. Be clear with speech. Listen to them first to help gain and understanding before leaping in. Don't make judgements, and try to listen to the feeling behind the words. Rather than the words itself.

Samaritans: Listening with people with Autism

Samaritans: Listening with people with Autism

Chapter 4 – User needs to be met on their level

Avoid talking down to the patient, and talk to them on their level. Avoid judgement, and be curteous and respectful.

Be reflective, and slow manner to help them understand.

Try to reassure, by sounding calm. If you are not doing this, this can cause anxiety.
Try to show consideration and tact.

Samaritans: Listening with people with Autism

Samaritans: Listening with people with Autism

Samaritans: Listening with people with Autism

Samaritans: Listening with people with Autism

Samaritans: Listening with people with Autism

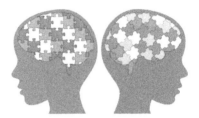

Samaritans: Listening with people with Autism

Samaritans: Listening with people with Autism

Samaritans: Listening with people with Autism

Samaritans: Listening with people with Autism

Samaritans: Listening with people with Autism

Samaritans: Listening with people with Autism

Samaritans: Listening with people with Autism

Samaritans: Listening with people with Autism

Samaritans: Listening with people with Autism

Samaritans: Listening with people with Autism

Samaritans: Listening with people with Autism

Samaritans: Listening with people with Autism

Samaritans: Listening with people with Autism

Samaritans: Listening with people with Autism

Samaritans: Listening with people with Autism

Samaritans: Listening with people with Autism

Samaritans: Listening with people with Autism

Chapter 5 – Coach them

Help them see things from your/someone else's points of view. People with Autism find it hard to see things from someone else's points of view.

Be reassuring and listen to what they have to say. People with Autism are highly intelligent but can become highly distressed if they feel. They are being spoken down to.

I have Autism and sometimes I feel that if I am not understood or listened to properly. This can cause obstacles.

Try to be there for them in times of distress.

Samaritans: Listening with people with Autism

Samaritans: Listening with people with Autism

Samaritans: Listening with people with Autism

Samaritans: Listening with people with Autism

Samaritans: Listening with people with Autism

Samaritans: Listening with people with Autism

Samaritans: Listening with people with Autism

Samaritans: Listening with people with Autism

Samaritans: Listening with people with Autism

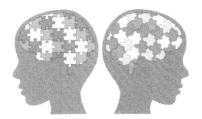

Samaritans: Listening with people with Autism

Chapter 6 – Show Empathy

Try showing empathy. Try showing them that you understand. Give them the benefit of the doubt. Try listening non judgementally.

Keep them distracted, in a positive way.

I just wanted to say also. That I know there is *more awareness* on Autism now than there used to be. However, I think there needs to be even more. I know people have spoken about those Autism shopping hours in supermarkets. However, in relation to Autism. What I can tell you that other people may not explain; Is that not only do I have the experience of hsving it. I have met thousands of people with it, met professionals, and have written pre existing books on it. I have medical qualifications and Autism training myself, and

Samaritans: Listening with people with Autism

what I am trying to say. Is that it's what you do on a practical and pragmatic basis. Sometimes over talking or over listening can be counterproductive. It's all about keeping them entertained and keeping them aware of their talents. Their skills, and their ambitions.

The way you listen is super important, and sometimes if you don't clarify something. This needs to be done.

I know you get training in The Samaritans anyway. Try to avoid hanging up, or if you have to go. Try explaining the reasons, and being positive, and confident along the way.

Printed in Great Britain
by Amazon